CW00566198

THIS BOOK BELONGS TO...

Name:	Age:

Favourite player:

2021/2022

My Predictions...	Actual...

Boro's final position:

Boro's top scorer:

Championship winners:

Championship top scorer:

FA Cup winners:

EFL Cup winners:

Contributors: Peter Rogers, Anthony Vickers

A TWOCAN PUBLICATION

©2021. Published by twocan under licence from Middlesbrough Football Club.

Every effort has been made to ensure the accuracy of information within this publication but the publishers cannot be held responsible for any errors or omissions. Views expressed are those of the authors and do not necessarily represent those of the publishers or the football club. All rights reserved.

ISBN: 978-1-914588-02-0

£9

CONTENTS

1. JOE LUMLEY

POSITION: Goalkeeper

DOB: 15/02/1995

COUNTRY: England

A summer signing from Queens Park Rangers, Joe started at Spurs alongside brother Billy who now runs a keeper academy in Australia. The pair honed their skills emulating former Boro keeper Shay Given.

Joe joined QPR in 2013 and after a string of lower league loan spells made his debut in 2016 then established himself as first choice the following year under former Boro boss Steve McClaren. At QPR he played behind Boro's Grant Hall.

2. ANFEREE DIJKSTEEL

POSITION: Defender

DOB: 27/10/1996

COUNTRY: Netherlands

The powerful Dutch defender came into professional football via the Nike Academy before moving to England with Charlton Athletic.

He won promotion with the Addicks via the League One Play-Offs then joined Boro in the summer of 2019. He suffered a serious knee injury early on but recovered to nail down a regular first-team place and was one of Boro's most consistent performers in 2020/21.

SQUAD 2021/22

4. GRANT HALL

POSITION: Defender

DOB: 29/10/1991

COUNTRY: England

The rock-solid defender was Neil Warnock's first Boro signing when he joined from Queens Park Rangers in August 2020. The Boro boss had already managed Grant at QPR, where the defender was Supporters' Player of the Year in 2015/16 and then captain.

After an injury-dogged start to his time at Boro he made his mark with strong tackles and a commanding aerial presence.

ISAIAH JONES

The side-foot pass is one of the most accurate passing techniques over shorter distances. The ability to find one of your teammates with a pass, even when under severe pressure, and retain possession of the ball is an essential factor in the way the game is played today.

SOCCER SKILLS

EXERCISE ONE

Set up a 10 x 10m grid. In one corner there are two players and on each of the other three corners there is one player.

Player A starts with the ball. Each player must pass the ball round the square in sequence then follow their pass. A passes to B then runs after his pass and takes up B's starting position. B passes to C and follows his pass to take C's position, and so on. All of the players must control the ball then pass it with the inside of their foot.

Key Factors

1. Non-kicking foot alongside the ball.
2. Pass with the inside of the foot.
3. Strike through the middle of the ball.
4. Keep your eyes on the ball and your head steady.

EXERCISE TWO

The set up is the same as exercise one.

In this exercise the players pass the ball in sequence, A through to D, but do not follow their pass, remaining stationary.

As soon as A plays the first pass, E sets off racing around the outside of the starting point. The players must pass the ball as quickly and accurately as possible while under pressure from E, who cannot tackle but is effectively racing the ball round the square.

The same key factors apply in this exercise as in the first, but the players are required to be able to pass the ball accurately while under pressure.

Any team who can retain possession through good accurate passing will always make it very difficult for the opposition. The side-foot pass is one of the most accurate passing techniques.

MARK SCHWARZER

Goalkeeper Mark Schwarzer arrived at Middlesbrough in February 1997 following a short spell with Bradford City. The giant Australian stopper played almost 450 games for Boro and gained the reputation as one of the best Premier League goalkeepers of all time.

An outstanding shot stopper, Schwarzer controlled his area with authority and was also comfortable with the ball at his feet. He made his Boro debut in the 1997 League Cup semi-final meeting with Stockport County and played in the Wembley final against Leicester City. He also played in the 1998 final against Chelsea before becoming a League Cup winner at the third attempt when Boro defeated Bolton 2-1 at the Millennium Stadium in 2004.

A key player throughout Steve McClaren's reign as Boro boss, Schwarzer also kept goal in Boro's 2006 UEFA Cup final appearance against Sevilla in Eindhoven.

BOROHEROES

VOICE

Charged with organising the defensive unit in front of him, goalkeeper Schwarzer would often be heard barking instructions to his teammates. With the whole pitch in his sight, it is an important part of the goalkeeper's role to advise teammates of the dangers he can spot.

EYES

Always keeping a close eye on the ball, goalkeeper Schwarzer used his sight to judge the flight of crosses and the speed of shots heading his way. Sight is a vital part of goalkeeping, particularly when quickly assessing whether to come for a ball or leave it for a defender.

FEET

The modern-day goalkeeper certainly needs to be comfortable with the ball at his feet. Mark Schwarzer was always alert and able to sprint off his line and clear danger with his feet, he was also happy to receive the ball from an under-pressure defence and clear the ball up-field.

HANDS

Blessed with the ability to quickly bring his hands into action to repel the opposition's efforts on goal, Schwarzer could always be relied upon to pull off saves and use his hands effectively to either gather the ball or push it to safety.

```
A G F G O L D E N G O A L A A V
O C L E A N S H E E T N T X O A
D R I B B L I N G A Y H B L U G
E B P H R N R U T F F Y U R C V
A F F H I T T H E W O O D W O R K M G
D I L C E N S X D T V R C G R G E O T S
B M A D J P Z E U I W J F N E A D E Z M
A R P K U L I E F S B M A M P I K O S R
L Q A T A T M S D O E M T R P J P Q P A
L Y V C P O A G O I D U A A I Y T N B I
S I W U E T G T A R N V B T K A H V W N
P R C L I N I C A L F I N I S H E R N B
E R Z N S T C H X M A M A M I E N L A O
C Q E H C N S H Y O S U J G L T U E M W
I O A F O S P T E W R O D B Z A M X T K
A J I N F F O X I N T H E B O X B F E I
L K A D E A N T Y V N R K B S Q I C G C
I M G F M U G I A N T K I L L I N G R K
S X P B U H E L G L O R T N O C L L A B
T H E B E A U T I F U L G A M E S P T T
```

SOCCER SEARCH

Ball Control	Clinical Finisher	Flip Flap	Hard Man	Rainbow Kick
Bicycle Kick	Cruyff Turn	Fox in the Box	Hit the Woodwork	Skipper
Boot it	Cup-tied	Gaffer	Magic Sponge	Target Man
Brace	Dead-ball Specialist	Giant-killing	Man On	The Beautiful Game
Clean Sheet	Dribbling	Golden Goal	Nutmeg	Treble

SQUAD 2021/22

6. DAEL FRY

POSITION: Defender

DOB: 30/08/1997

COUNTRY: England

Boro-born Dael has been with the club since the age of seven. The towering 6ft4 centre-back won the World Cup with England as an Under-20 and the Toulon Tournament as an Under-21.

He made his Boro debut in 2015 and has since become a fixture at the back impressing with both his no-nonsense defending and an ability to read the game and carry the ball out from the back.

7. MARCUS TAVERNIER

POSITION: Midfielder

DOB: 22/03/1999

COUNTRY: England

The speedy and skilful Academy graduate made his first-team bow in August 2017 just days after scoring a hat-trick for the Under-23s against Norwich.

The livewire midfielder further showed his goalscoring credentials with strikes against Bournemouth and Sunderland that first season and has since flourished with eye-catching displays both on the flanks and through the middle.

8. ONEL HERNANDEZ

POSITION: Attacker

DOB: 01/02/1993

COUNTRY: Cuba

The flying winger has twice won promotion to the Premier League with Norwich and Neil Warnock hopes he can do the same while on loan at Boro.

He was born in Cuba but moved to Germany at the age of six and played for Arminia Bielefeld, Wolfsburg and Eintracht Braunschweig before switching to Norwich in January 2018. He made his Canaries debut against Boro and later became the first Cuban to play in the Premier League.

CLASSIC

FANTASTIC

Roary the Lion is hiding in the crowd in five places.

Can you find him?

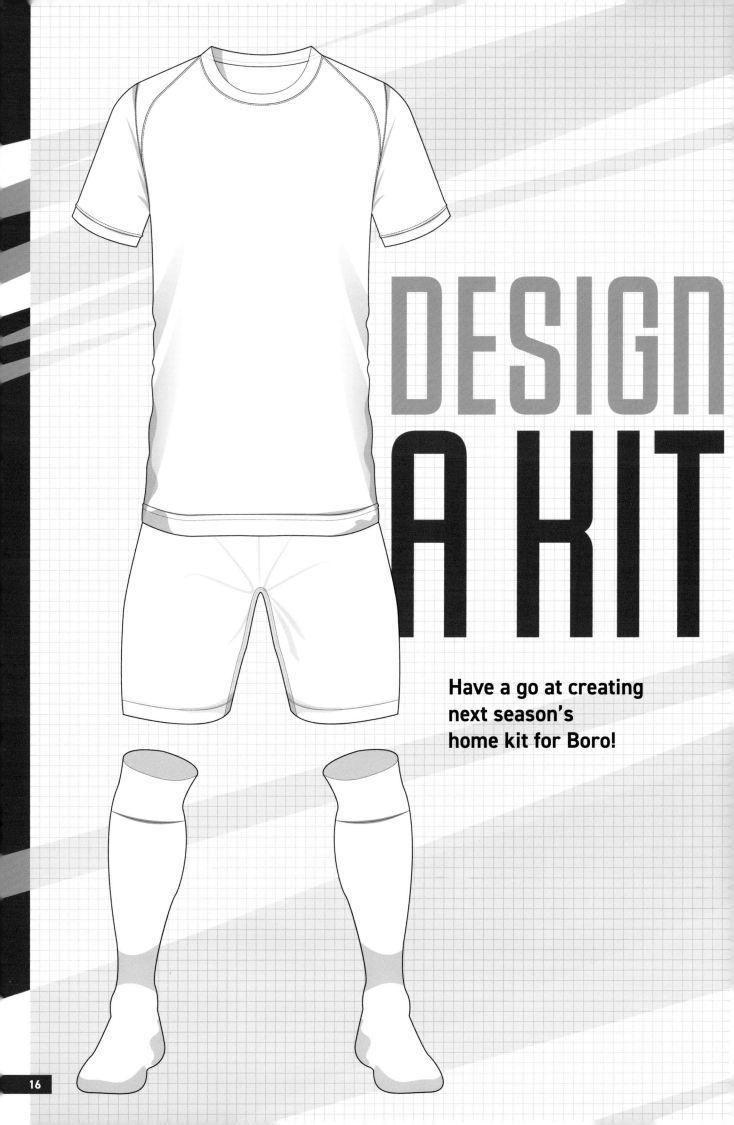

DESIGN A KIT

Have a go at creating next season's home kit for Boro!

ANFERNEE
DIJKSTEEL

Middlesbrough's proud red and white colours have been a long held tradition at both Ayresome Park and the Riverside Stadium. However, excitement and anticipation still surrounds the launch of every new Boro kit.

Each and every playing strip forms its own part of Middlesbrough history and supporters young and old will all have their own favourites. Let's take a look back at four of the best...

1987/88

Boro had a new look for their 1987/88 Second Division campaign as kit manufacturer Skill produced their first strip for the club. The red shirt had a chequered pattern to the material with a series of white horizontal stripes across the chest area.

Housed within the white striped section was the club crest and club's MFC initials plus the sponsor's branding. The shirt had a white v-neck collar with red trim - a theme that was repeated on the cuffs.

The white shorts had red flashes at the bottom of the side panels, while the all-red socks were topped with two white bands.

DRESSED TO IMPRESS

Under the management of Bruce Rioch, Middlesbrough completed a memorable back-to-back promotion as the club secured a return to the top flight.

The team boasted the best defensive record in the second tier in 1987/88 and were equally as efficient at the attacking end of the pitch too - a fact demonstrated with a 6-0 mauling of Sheffield United in April 1988. After ending the regulation season in third place Boro defeated Chelsea 2-1 on aggregate in the end-of-season Play-Offs.

HE WORE IT WELL

Dean Glover enjoyed an impressive first season with Boro in 1987/88 following a £60,000 summer switch from Aston Villa.

With the ability to operate at both right-back and in a defensive midfield role, Glover became a key man in the Boro side, making 40 appearances and scoring twice.

In 1993 the club began a longstanding partnership with Italian kit manufacturer Errea who produced their first Boro kit for the club's farewell season at Ayresome Park.

A neat all-red shirt had a trendy button section to the dark blue collar area. The club crest, Errea motif and sponsor's logo were all situated on the chest area. The blue collar had a red and white trim and this theme was used on the cuffs of the shirt too.

The predominately white shorts carried an attractive blue and red patterned section on the side panels with the club crest and Errea branding on the front. The solid red socks were topped with a blue band and carried the Errea motif on the shin pad area.

DRESSED TO IMPRESS

Middlesbrough signed off from life at Ayresome Park in style as Bryan Robson's side were crowned Division One champions in 1994/95.

Boro ended their 92-year stay at Ayresome Park with a 2-1 win over Luton Town in their final home game of the season to secure top spot and the only automatic promotion place that season.

HE WORE IT WELL

Scottish forward John Hendrie was one of many star performers in Boro's 1994/95 title-winning season.

Signed from Leeds United in 1990, Hendrie netted 17 goals in 1994/95, 15 of which came in the league and included the final goal at Ayresome Park that saw him granted legendary status on Teesside.

1994/95

ALL KITTED OUT

9. UCHE IKPEAZU

POSITION: Striker

DOB: 28/02/1995

COUNTRY: Uganda

The powerful Harrow-born frontman started at Watford then joined Crewe, Port Vale and Blackpool on loan before signing for Cambridge United. He had a spell at Hearts and played in the 2019 Scottish Cup final before joining Wycombe.

He signed for Boro this summer. Uche has a FIFA strength rating of 94, one of the highest in the whole game. He was called up for Uganda in March 2020 but the games were postponed because of Covid-19.

10. MARTIN PAYERO

POSITION: Midfielder

DOB: 11/09/1998

COUNTRY: Argentina

Martin, another summer signing, arrived as one of the most highly-rated young players in Argentina after featuring for his national side in the Tokyo Olympics.

He caught the eye with his athleticism, dribbling and dead-ball delivery as his club Banfield reached the final of the Diego Maradona Cup - a replacement competition after the 2020 Premera Division was scrapped due to Covid-19.

SQUAD 2021/22

11. ANDRAZ SPORAR

POSITION: Striker

DOB: 27/02/1994

COUNTRY: Slovenia

Slovenian star striker Sporar joined Boro on deadline day from Sporting Lisbon, initially on loan.

The lively frontman is a serial winner. He has won league titles in three countries: in Switzerland with Basel, in Slovakia with Slovan Bratislava and last season in Portugal he won the title with Sporting and the cup in a loan spell at Braga. Andraz has played over 300 senior games and scored 141 goals. He won the Slovakian Golden Boot two years in a row.

12. MARCUS BROWNE

POSITION: Midfielder

DOB: 18/12/1997

COUNTRY: England

The London-born winger started at the West Ham Academy and had loan spells at Wigan and Oxford before joining Boro in the summer of 2019.

After a rocky start to his first season he was loaned back to Oxford where he won rave reviews as they reached the League One Play-Off final. Back at Boro he has featured on the flank and through the middle.

Footballers are fit, fast, powerful and agile and that doesn't come easily. Only the most talented young players get signed by clubs and only the most driven of those make it to the top. Commitment is crucial to help talent shine and to be their best, players must put in the hard yards in all weathers.

Training is meticulously planned. Sessions earlier in the week focus on recovery from the previous game. Midweek gets intense with the emphasis on strength, speed, and skills. And training takes a tactical turn as matchday looms.

A 'normal' Boro week starts on Sunday, the day after the match, with a gentle morning warm-down of jogging or cycling - although squad players who didn't feature face a tougher work-out.

Monday has one eye on recovery with a light football session in the morning, maybe first touch, and gentle gym work in the afternoon. Every player has their own personal training plan to develop key muscle groups.

Tuesday is more intense with small-sided games, keep-ball exercises and man-marking drills while in the afternoon there may be a strength session in the gym with weights, squats and pull-ups.

It goes up a gear on Wednesday with an 11-a-side session working on the tactical shape for Saturday's opposition while the afternoon could be gruelling, explosive sprint work.

Thursday is a rest day – phew! - and Friday is geared to specific match tactics, set-plays and crossing or shooting. There is a team meeting to talk about the opposition with video footage of their weaknesses. Then it is the match!

Training is demanding so refuelling is crucial to keep players physically strong and mentally sharp. Nutrition and hydration is vital. Players eat lots of fresh fruit and vegetables, cut out the chocolate and crisps and drink plenty of water. Boro have a special chef at the Rockliffe training ground to make sure the squad have tasty and nutritious mid-day and matchday meals.

Recovery is important too. That means a good night's sleep. Some clubs even have 'sleep coaches' to help players relax and nod off. Healthy food and solid sleep is a basic building block for aspiring footballers. Get into those good habits and train properly and the sky is the limit.

TRAIN LIKE A PRO

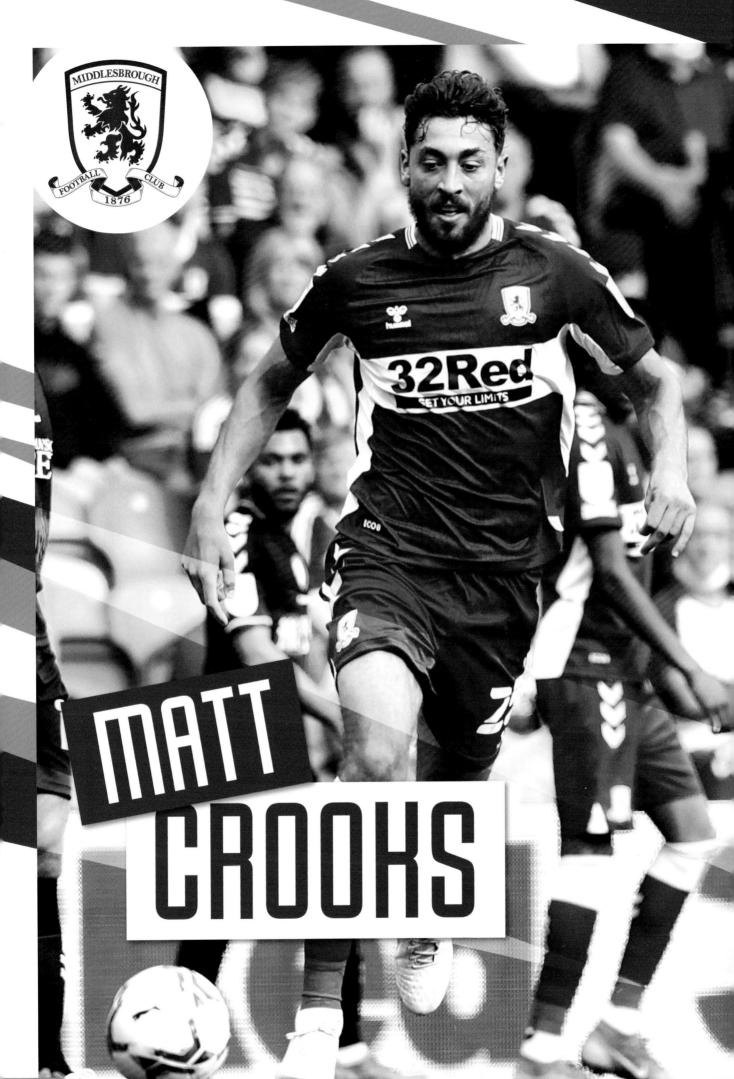

MATT
CROOKS

It has been said that dribbling is a dying art. The pace of the modern game makes it more difficult, but there are players about, even in today's lightning fast conditions, who have the confidence to keep hold of the ball and take on defenders.

SOCCER SKILLS

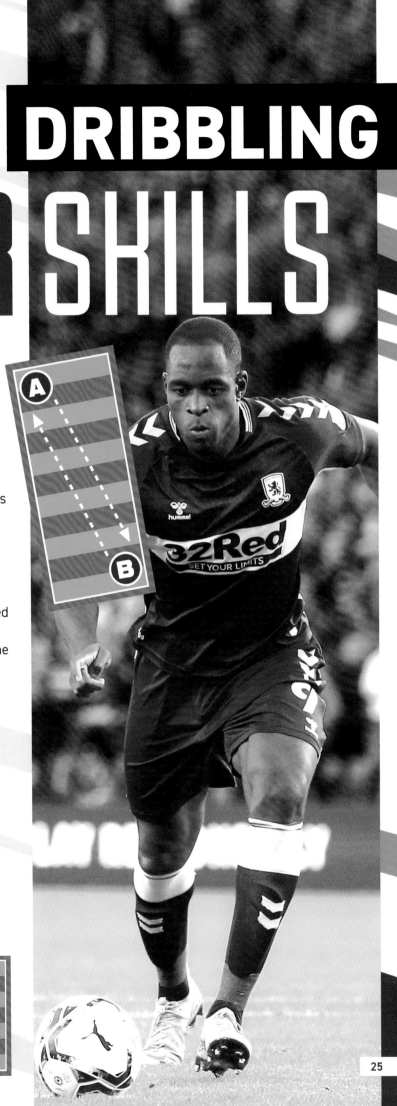

DRIBBLING

EXERCISE ONE

As a warm-up exercise, players A and B each dribble a ball around a 20 x 10m grid, avoiding each other, but staying within the grid boundary lines.

They progress to a 'cat and mouse' race between the corners - the player with the most visits to each corner wins the race. One of the main problems in this exercise is avoiding the other player, and their ball.

EXERCISE TWO

Now for a more realistic exercise. Six players are used as shown, with three attackers and three defenders at any one time. When play starts, the players with the ball attack any of the three opposing goals, changing their target as they choose. The defenders have, simply, to stop their opposite number from scoring, but must not interfere with any other pair.

Key Factors

1. Close control.
2. Quick change of direction.
3. Acceleration away from defender.
4. Feints, to wrong-foot defender.
5. Head up to see the whole picture.

When the defenders win possession, they become the attackers, and go for goal themselves. This can be a very enjoyable practice, but also quite tiring.

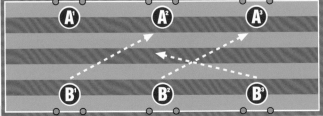

ANSWER

1

2

ANSWER

3

ANSWER

4

ANSWER

5

ANSWER

GUESS
THE CLUB

6
ANSWER

7
ANSWER

8
ANSWER

9
ANSWER

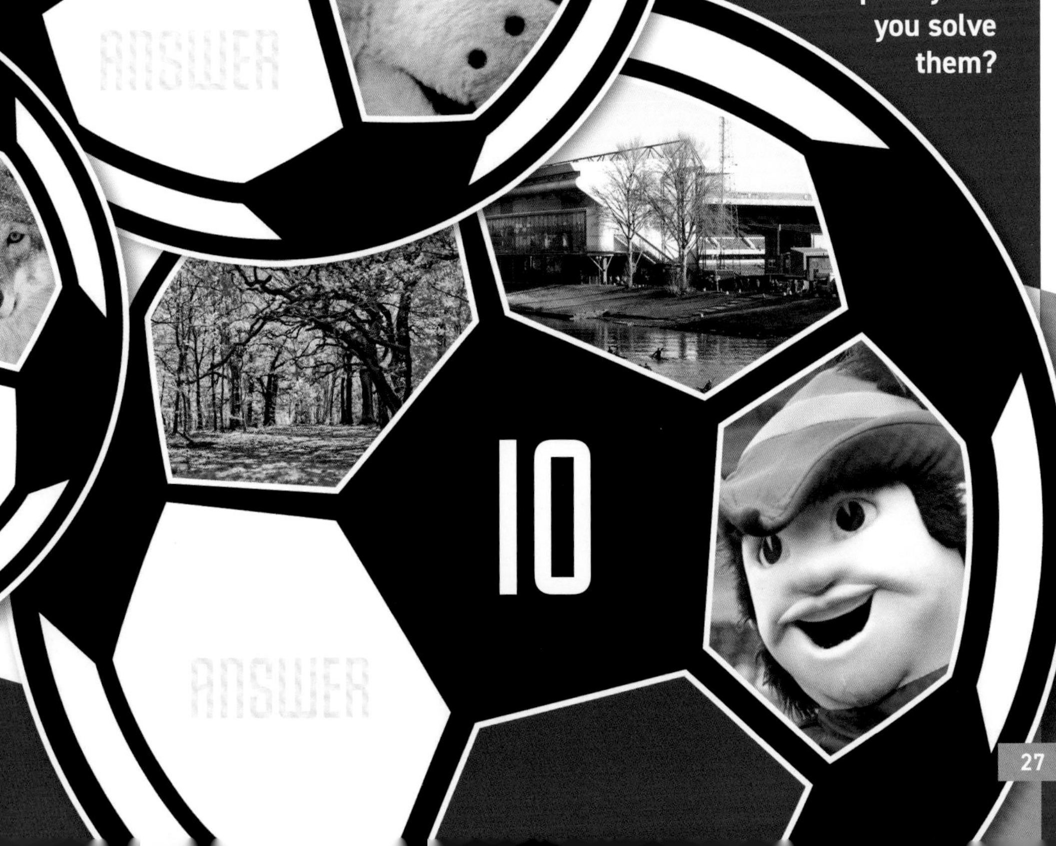

10
ANSWER

Each football holds the clues to the identity of a Premier League or Football League club, how quickly can you solve them?

ANSWERS ON PAGE 62

14. LEE PELTIER

POSITION: Defender

DOB: 11/12/1986

COUNTRY: England

Experienced defender Lee started at home-town club Liverpool and played for the first team in both the League Cup and Champions League before leaving for Yeovil in 2008.

He had spells at Huddersfield, Leicester and Leeds then joined Cardiff where he was a key player in the team Neil Warnock led to a Premier League promotion. He joined Boro this summer after his deal at West Bromwich Albion ended.

SQUAD 2021/22

16. JONNY HOWSON

POSITION: Midfielder

DOB: 21/05/1988

COUNTRY: England

Utility man Jonny joined Boro from Norwich in July 2017 with an impressive Championship CV having captained both the Canaries in their promotion campaign and home-town club Leeds before that.

The energetic midfielder, a former England Under-21 international, has played in a host of positions for Boro including centre-back, wing-back and No 10.

GOAL
OF THE SEASON

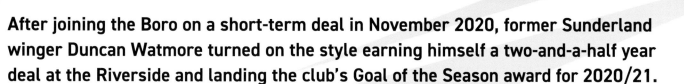

DUNCAN WATMORE
V HUDDERSFIELD TOWN · FEBRUARY 2021

After joining the Boro on a short-term deal in November 2020, former Sunderland winger Duncan Watmore turned on the style earning himself a two-and-a-half year deal at the Riverside and landing the club's Goal of the Season award for 2020/21.

When it came to voting for Boro's best goal of the season, fans gave Watmore's mazy dribble and emphatic finish in the 2-1 home victory over Huddersfield Town in February 2021 their seal of approval. On an eventful evening at the Riverside, the hosts fell behind inside the opening ten minutes when Isaac Mbenza whipped home a 25-yard free-kick for the Terriers.

However, Watmore then stole the show with a wonderful equaliser as he left two defenders in his wake with a skilful display of dribbling ability before then exquisitely curling the ball past visiting 'keeper Ryan Schofield. Had supporters have been in attendance, the Riverside would have erupted with delight.

The goal provided Boro with the platform to go on and win the match. Ashley Fletcher fired Boro in front form the penalty-spot on the stroke of half-time but the team had to dig in and show great character to secure the three points after ending the game with ten men following the controversial sending off of Paddy McNair.

Watmore's solo strike in this victory over Huddersfield gave Neil Warnock's men their first win in six matches and was the winger's sixth goal of a nine-goal campaign.

Another goal to come strongly into the reckoning for the Goal of the Season title was left-back Marc Bola's sizzling strike against Reading. February was clearly the month for great Boro goals with Bola's effort coming just four days after Watmore's wonder strike. Bola's rare strike doubled Boro's lead at Reading as Warnock's side wrapped up another three points on the road.

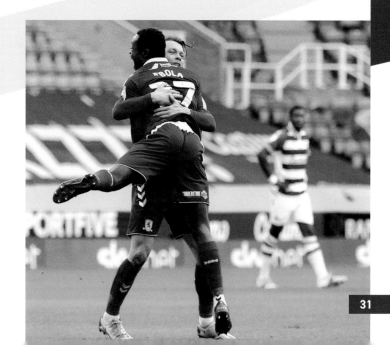

Australian international striker Mark Viduka scored an impressive 42 goals in just 103 appearances for Middlesbrough between 2004 and 2007.

Viduka was signed by Steve McClaren from Leeds United for a fee of £4.5M in the summer of 2004 as Boro bolstered their squad ahead of the 2004/05 campaign that would see the team competing on both a domestic and European front.

The Australian added a real physical presence to the Boro attack and in his second season with the club his goals helped Boro reach the League Cup quarter-final, FA Cup semi-final and the UEFA Cup final. His final season at the Riverside was his most productive in terms of goals - he weighed in with 19 of which 14 were in the Premier League.

MARK VIDUKA

BOROHEROES

HEADERS

A good number of Mark Viduka's Boro goals came from headers. A real threat in the air, Viduka had the power to out-jump defenders and then use his head to direct the ball past the 'keeper and into the net. Once the ball was in and around the six-yard box and in the air there was always a good chance he would head it home.

ENCOURAGEMENT

As the focal point of the attack, Viduka could be relied upon to advise and encourage teammates to play the ball into areas where he could be most effective and cause danger to the opposition.

CHEST CONTROL

As a strong centre-forward who led the Middlesbrough attack so well, Mark Viduka was blessed with a great ability to play with his back to goal and take the ball under control on his chest. He could then hold up play while others arrived in support or lay the ball off to a teammate.

GOALS

Although a fair amount of Viduka's impressive 42 goals for Boro came from headers, he was pretty lethal with a trusty right foot too. With the ability to take shots first time or while on the run - when Viduka pulled the trigger with his right foot it rarely let him down.

DAEL FRY

MOST INTERNATIONAL CAPS

Australian goalkeeper Mark Schwarzer won more international caps as a Middlesbrough player than anyone else. The popular 'keeper won almost 50 percent of his international caps for the Socceroos while plying his club trade at the Riverside.

Schwarzer made his international debut back in 1994 and went on to mass 109 appearances for his country, 52 of which were as a Middlesbrough player. He represented the Socceroos at both the 2006 and 2010 World Cup finals.

It was Schwarzer's impressive club form that under-pinned his place as Australia's first choice 'keeper for so long. During a 445-game Boro career that spanned from 1997 to 2008, Schwarzer appeared in three League Cup finals for Boro and also the UEFA Cup final in 2006. He remains widely regarded as one of the club's finest goalkeepers.

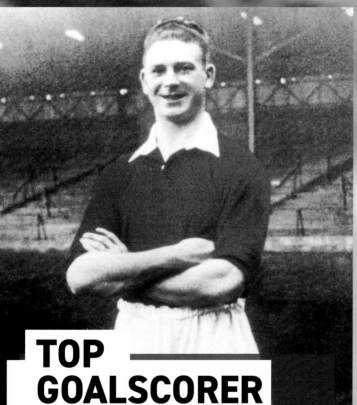

TOP GOALSCORER

Ace marksman George Camsell holds the record as Middlesbrough Football Club's record goalscorer. Plucked from Durham City in 1925, Camsell went on to net a phenomenal 345 goals in 453 games for Boro.

His 59 league goals in the 1926/27 season remain a club record that is unlikely to ever be surpassed. Incredibly, his 59-goal haul in 1926/27 included nine hat-tricks! A proud Football League record that remains intact to this day.

Unsurprisingly, Camsell's goalscoring form at Ayresome Park won him international recognition with England where he fired home 18 goals in just nine appearances. A true Middlesbrough legend, Camsell sadly died in 1966, aged 63, and there is a suite named after him at the Riverside Stadium.

YOUNGEST PLAYER

Defender Nathan Wood is Boro's youngest-ever first team player. The hot prospect came off the bench to replace Dani Ayala after 62 minutes in a 3-3 Carabao Cup draw with Notts County on August 14, 2018. He was aged just 16 years and 75 days and his moment of history came just a week after the Conyers School pupil picked up his GCSE results!

Centre-back Wood, who grew up in Ingleby Barwick, has since played 12 times for Boro and had a loan spell at League One outfit Crewe Alexandra. This season he is on loan at Hibernian in Scotland. The previous record holder was striker Luke Williams, who made his debut in a Championship game at Barnsley aged 16 and 200 days back in December 2009.

RECORD MAKERS

A selection of players, games, facts and figures which all shape the club's proud history.

RECORD POINTS HAUL

Middlesbrough recorded their best points haul in a league campaign when Bruce Rioch's side won promotion from the Third Division in 1986/87. Boro amassed a club record 94 points as they secured promotion as Third Division runners-up, missing out on the title to AFC Bournemouth who ended the campaign with 97. The team won 28 of their 46 Third Division games, drew ten and suffered only eight defeats in what was a special season at Ayresome Park.

The team's success was spearheaded by the goals of Bernie Slaven who topped the club's scoring charts with 21 goals, 17 of which came in the league. The emergence of Tony Mowbray and Gary Pallister as central defenders provided the rock that the Boro defence would be built upon as the club went on to enjoy back-to-back promotions under Rioch and a return to the top flight just 12 months later.

RECORD ATTENDANCE

As we all know, there are few better places to be than inside a packed Riverside Stadium and cheering Neil Warnock's team on to victory. The club moved from its former home at Ayresome Park to the Riverside in 1995 and the record attendance for a Boro match at the new ground was set on Wednesday, 5 March 2003 when 34,814 fans saw Geremi score the only goal of the game as Boro defeated Newcastle United under the lights in the Premier League.

Ironically, the record attendance for a match at Ayresome Park was also set for a league match with Newcastle. A whopping 53,802 fans were shoehorned into the famous old ground to see Boro complete a top-flight double over the Magpies on 27 December 1949.

SQUAD 2021/22

17. PADDY McNAIR

POSITION: Midfielder/defender

DOB: 27/04/1995

COUNTRY: Northern Ireland

The former Manchester United man arrived at the Riverside from Sunderland in June 2018 as an attacking midfielder but made his Boro breakthrough as a right wing-back.

Since then the Northern Ireland international he has made as many appearances as a composed and cultured central defender as in his more natural role in the engine room. He has a cracking dead-ball delivery.

18. DUNCAN WATMORE

POSITION: Striker

DOB: 08/03/1994

COUNTRY: England

The high-energy frontman with an eye for goal has bounced back from TWO cruciate injuries to rebuild his career. After his contract ended at Sunderland he trained and played for free at Boro to prove his fitness before signing a deal in November 2020.

With some lively displays along the way he finished the season as top scorer with nine goals in 29 games. Brainy Duncan has a first class university degree in economics and business management.

20. DARNELL FISHER

POSITION: Defender

DOB: 04/04/1994

COUNTRY: England

Rapid right-back Darnell has been ruled out of the first phase of the 2021/22 season after suffering a freak knee injury over the summer.

He joined from Preston in January 2021 and quickly impressed. Darnell started at Celtic after being spotted playing junior football in his home town of Reading. He won the League and League Cup with the Scottish giants before spells at St Johnstone and Rotherham.

21. SAMMY AMEOBI

POSITION: Midfielder

DOB: 01/05/1992

COUNTRY: England

Sammy signed for Boro in the summer from Nottingham Forest, nine years after a loan spell at the Riverside as a youngster. The towering and tricky winger made his debut for home-town club Newcastle in 2011 alongside his older brother, striker Shola.

He had also played at Cardiff City and Bolton Wanderers before Forest. Sammy played at international level for Nigeria Under-20s and England Under-21s.

IMPOSSIBLE Footy Decisions

Would you rather...

have to play the rest of your football games in 35 degree heat or a blizzard?

Would you rather...

have Uche Ikpeazu's ability to score goals or Joe Lumley's ability to save them?

Would you rather...

have a pause button or a rewind button for your life?

Would you rather...

have unlimited battery life on all your devices or free wifi wherever you go?

Would you rather...

run 100 laps of the pitch or complete 200 burpees?

Would you rather...

score the FA Cup final winning goal against Sunderland in your only game for Middlesbrough or play 300 games for Boro in League One?

Would you rather...

be remembered for a terrible footy howler or be forgotten completely?

Would you rather...

sell your best player to Newcastle United for £50m or sell him abroad for £20m?

Would you rather...

have to take a penalty against Joe Lumley or have Duncan Watmore take a penalty against you?

Would you rather...

sit right at the back during a game or have the best seats in the stadium, but not be allowed to eat, drink or use the bathroom?

Would you rather...

be the star in League Two
Or a squad player
in the Premier League?

Would you rather...

Middlesbrough win the FA Cup
or England win the World Cup?

Would you rather...

your match superstition be wearing
the same socks for a season Or the
same underwear for a month?

Would you rather...

lose on television or
win with nobody watching?

Would you rather...

have a long, average playing career or have
a short, fantastic career cut short by injury?

Would you rather...

lose to Leeds United twice
and finish top or beat them
twice and finish bottom?

Would you rather...

clean the dressing room
toilet with your toothbrush
or the floor with your tongue?

Would you rather...

play only five minutes
for Boro or win the
Premier League
with the Magpies?

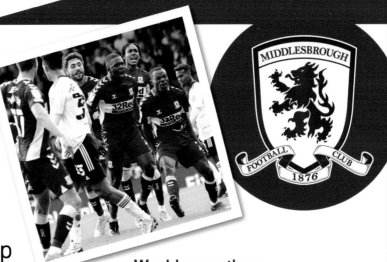

Would you rather...

have to wear every shirt inside out
or every pair of pants backwards?

Would you rather...

give up your mobile phone for
a month or bathing for a month?

Would you rather...

be alone all your life or surrounded
by Sunderland supporters?

Would you rather...
play for
Middlesbrough and
always lose Or sit On
the bench and Boro
always win?

Would you rather...

the half-time menu got rid of pies or pop?

Would you rather...

become a legendary manager
or a legendary player?

39

GRANT HALL

Captain of Middlesbrough's 2004 League Cup winning team, defender Gareth Southgate became Steve McClaren's first signing as Boro boss when he joined the club from Aston Villa in July 2001.

Across a five-season period Southgate made over 200 appearances at the heart of the Boro defence and after just one season at the club he was appointed captain. He became the first skipper to lead Boro to a major domestic cup triumph when they won the 2004 League Cup.

A mainstay of the side which reached the 2006 UEFA Cup final, Southgate was named Boro manager following Steve McClaren's elevation to England manager - a role Southgate would of course go on to successfully hold himself.

GARETH SOUTHGATE

BORO HEROES

TEMPERAMENT

Often faced with containing dangerous forwards, Gareth Southgate had the perfect mindset for defending. He very rarely lost concentration and always kept his cool. In the heat of any on-field duel, Southgate kept his mind on the task in hand and more often than not came out on top in one-on-one situations.

RALLYING CALL

Handed the captain's armband by Steve McClaren, Southgate's ability to lead and inspire his teammates was there for all to see. Always there with an encouraging call to those around him, Southgate led by example and was never afraid to let players know if standards were dropped.

PASSING SKILLS

Always comfortable with the ball at his feet, Southgate was an accomplished ball-playing defender who could always be relied upon to bring the ball out of defence and help the side turn defence to attack.

QUICK ON HIS HEELS

Gareth Southgate was always alive and alert to danger and when it occurred he was quick on his heels to track and tackle opponents. Not only was he swift over the ground but he was also quick to leap and win headed duels too.

1996/97

Boro had a striking look for the eventful 1996/97 season at the Riverside as Errea produced a classic Middlesbrough kit that lives long in the memory.

The red shirt had the word 'Boro' worked into the fabric and running down the right-hand half of the shirt. A white v-neck collar with a red and black trim had a red panel woven into the base of the collar to give the impression of being a round-necked shirt. The sponsor's logo sat in the centre of the shirt with the Errea branding on the chest area but the club crest was uniquely placed on the sleeve of the left arm.

The white shirts also had the club name 'Boro' printed in red on the right leg of the shorts with the Errea logo on the opposite side. The all red socks had one thin white band at the top with club crest and Errea branding on the shin pad area.

DRESSED TO IMPRESS

Middlesbrough certainly make their mark on the biggest of stages in this classic Boro kit as Bryan Robson's side enjoyed a Wembley double by reaching both the League Cup and FA Cup finals.

Sadly the team were unable to land a major piece of silverware, after drawing 1-1 with Leicester City in the League Cup final at Wembley, they slipped to a narrow 1-0 defeat in the Hillsborough replay. While finally overcoming giant-killing Chesterfield in the FA Cup semi-final, Robson's men were edged out by Chelsea at the final hurdle.

HE WORE IT WELL

A sensational signing from Juventus, striker Fabrizio Ravanelli fired home an incredible 31 goals for Boro in 48 appearances in the 1996/97 season.

The Italian marked his Boro debut with an opening-day Premier League hat-trick against Liverpool and that set the tone for the season ahead. His 15 goals in cup competitions were vital in the team's run to both domestic cup finals with Ravanelli on target in the League Cup final match with Leicester City at Wembley.

In something of a throwback to Middlesbrough shirts of the past, the club's 2005/06 kit offering had a familiar large white band across the chest area.

The white band was used to house the sponsor's branding with the club crest and Errea logo sitting above. The shirt was topped with a red v-neck collar with white trim and white cuffs.

A classy pair of all-red shorts were enhanced with a thin white trim at the bottom and on the side panels. The socks were predominantly red with 'MFC' on the shin pad area and topped with a black and white band that also showed the Errea motif.

DRESSED TO IMPRESS

Having qualified for the UEFA Cup after ending the previous season seventh in the Premier League, Boro attacked their 2005/06 campaign in pursuit of both domestic and European glory.

Under the guidance of Steve McClaren, the team reached the FA Cup semi-finals and League Cup quarter-finals, however it was in the UEFA Cup where the drama really unfolded. Boro enjoyed a never-to-be-forgotten run to the UEFA Cup final which included a dramatic 4-3 aggregate semi-final victory over Steaua Bucharest.

HE WORE IT WELL

In what was his first season at the Riverside, following a £7.5M move from Portsmouth, Yakubu topped the Boro scoring charts in 2005/06.

The powerful Nigerian striker scored 19 goals, 13 of which came in the Premier League, four in the FA Cup and two in the UEFA Cup campaign including a penalty against Roma in the last 16 as Boro progressed en route to facing Sevilla in the final.

2005/06

ALL KITTED OUT

SQUAD 2021/22

22. SOL BAMBA

POSITION: Defender
DOB: 13/01/1985
COUNTRY: Ivory Coast

Neil Warnock wanted his former promotion winning Cardiff skipper at Boro to add experience on the pitch and in the dressing room. The defender, now 36, is fighting fit again after a serious illness.

He was born in France and has played for PSG and for top flight teams in Scotland, Turkey and Italy and has won 46 caps for Ivory Coast. In England he has had successful spells with Leicester, Leeds and has been a fans' favourite at them all.

23. JAMES LEA SILIKI

POSITION: Midfielder
DOB: 12/06/1996
COUNTRY: Cameroon

Pass master Siliki arrived on deadline day in a loan move from French club Rennes. The France-born Cameroon international started in the PSG Academy but made his big breakthrough at Rennes.

The schemer was a key man as they qualified for the Champions League in 2020 where he played against Arsenal and Chelsea and he scored in the penalty shoot-out when they shocked PSG to win the French cup in 2019.

24. CONNOR MALLEY

POSITION: Midfielder
DOB: 20/03/2000
COUNTRY: England

The Newcastle-born midfielder started at the Sunderland Academy before switching to the Boro set-up in 2016. He has battled through the age groups at Boro to win a professional deal and broke through into the first team with a few cameo outings last season.

The highly-rated youngster has also had loan spells at Scottish side Ayr United and then Carlisle.

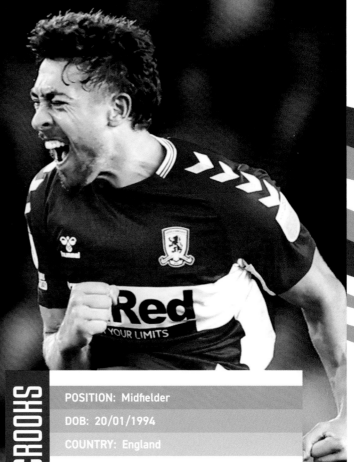

25. MATT CROOKS

POSITION: Midfielder
DOB: 20/01/1994
COUNTRY: England

Man-mountain midfielder Matt - an imposing six foot four - joined Boro in the summer from Rotherham to add some steel.

He can play anywhere across the midfield and chips in with goals too: he got 21 in 97 games at Rotherham as he helped them to promotion in 2019/20. After starting in the Manchester United Academy he has had spells at Accrington Stanley, Glasgow Rangers and Northampton Town.

MARCUS TAVERNIER

One of a player's greatest assets is the ability to win the ball. The following exercise can be used to improve a player's tackling abilities.

TACKLING SKILLS

SOCCER

EXERCISE

Set up a 10m x 20m grid.

In this two-on-two exercise, the aim of the game is to score a goal by taking the ball past the two opposing defenders, to the end line, and stand on the ball. The defenders just have to stop them.

As well as producing plenty of opportunities for the defenders to tackle, this session will test the defenders' abilities to work together, and communicate.

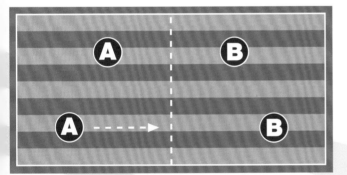

Key Factors

1. **Be patient - do not dive in.**

2. **Stay on your feet if possible.**

3. **Time the tackle with bodyweight behind it.**

4. **Be determined to win it.**

The reason that great players win so many tackles is not just because they know how to tackle and have good technique, it is because they have big hearts and are determined to win their challenges on the pitch.

47

ODDBALLS

ANSWERS ON PAGE 62

Three of the four pictures in each football represent a Premier League or Football League club, can you figure out the football club as well as the odd one out?

1

B C D A

ANSWER

2

A B C D 1898

ANSWER

3

C B A D

ANSWER

4

C FOOTBALL CLUB B A D

ANSWER

5

B A C D

ANSWER

PLAYER
OF THE SEASON

PADDY McNAIR

Boro's Northern Ireland international defender Paddy McNair was the fans' overwhelming choice for the club's coveted Player of the Season accolade at the end of the 2020/21 Championship campaign.

The Ballyclare-born central defender, who began his career with Manchester United and joined Boro from Sunderland in the summer of 2018, enjoyed a standout season under the management of Neil Warnock.

McNair made 47 appearances in all competitions for Boro last season and his solid performances, coupled with his clam ability on the ball, saw the Riverside faithful vote him the club's star performer for 2020/21. He was consistently praised for his contribution by his manager and found himself on the scoresheet twice - once in the home draw with Cardiff City and again in the 3-0 rout of Stoke City at the Riverside.

In a season where Boro competed at the business end of the table and fought bravely for a Play-Off spot, McNair's defensive experience plus his vision and passing were a key factor in what was a positive campaign at the Riverside.

The 26-year-old was ever-present in Boro's Championship campaign and with him at the heart of the defence again in 2021/22 there will be a real belief that the team can improve on last season's tenth-placed finish.

MARC BOLA

In what was his second season at the club, Marc Bola established himself at the team's first choice left-back and his impressive contribution to Boro's 2020/21 campaign saw him voted runner-up in the end-of-season Player of the Season poll.

The Greenwich-born former Arsenal man made 41 Championship appearances for Boro last season and appears all set to be one of the first names on Neil Warnock's teamsheet in 2021/22.

DAEL FRY

Academy graduate Dael Fry landed third spot in the Boro's Player of the Season voting following another impressive campaign with his hometown club.

The England U21 international formed an excellent central defensive partnership with Paddy McNair and scored his first league goal for the club in February 2021, a month before his season was ended due to injury. A fully fit Fry will certainly be a big boost for Boro's plans for the new campaign.

MARTIN PAYERO

COLOUR
JONNY
HOWSON

SQUAD 2021/22

27. MARC BOLA

POSITION: Defender

DOB: 09/12/1997

COUNTRY: England

The popular attacking left-back made a goalscoring start to the season with a late leveller in a 1-1 draw at Fulham on the first weekend.

He was just picking up where he left off after a sizzling first full season under Neil Warnock as his tough tackling and assertive overlaps made him a first-team fixture. He joined Boro from Blackpool in the summer of 2019 but was loaned back after a sticky start.

28. LUKE DANIELS

POSITION: Goalkeeper

DOB: 05/01/1988

COUNTRY: England

A solid second string shot-stopper, well-travelled Luke has played in all four tiers of the English professional game and the Scottish Premier League too.

He started at top-flight West Bromwich Albion and had loan spells at seven clubs before a three year stint at Scunthorpe. He joined Boro this summer from Brentford after helping the Bees win promotion to the Premier League.

35. ISAIAH JONES

POSITION: Midfielder

DOB: 26/06/1999

COUNTRY: England

The speedy youngster impressed from the bench in his league debut as he helped tee-up the equaliser at Fulham in the opening weekend.

The highly-rated winger, born in London, joined Boro from non-league Tooting and Mitcham in May 2019 and has since had loan spells in Scotland with St Johnstone and Queen of the South.

1. WHO AM I?

I progressed though the Boro Academy and into the club's first team

I played as a wide attacking midfielder

I made my Boro debut against Ipswich Town in 2002

After leaving the club in 2009, I have since returned for a second spell as a Boro player

I won 35 caps for England during my career

3. WHO AM I?

I joined the Boro Academy at the age of 12

I made my first team debut for the club in 2011

I was loaned to three lower division clubs in the early part of my Boro career

I played in all 38 of Boro's 2016/17 Premier League fixtures

I won promotion to the Premier League with my current club last season

GUESS WHO

2. WHO AM I?

I was born in Ireland in 1987

I began my career with Charlton Athletic

I joined Middlesbrough in the summer of 2017 in a big money transfer

In 2018/19 I was voted into the Championship Team of the Season

I have amassed half a century of international caps for the Republic of Ireland

I was born in
Middlesbrough in 1967

I twice helped Boro win
promotion to the top flight

In 249 games I scored 26
league goals for the club

My form for Boro was
rewarded with eight caps
for England at U21 level

After leaving Ayresome Park
I became a Premier League
winner with my next club

4. WHO AM I?

I made my Middlesbrough
debut back in 1982

I was aged just 22 when
I became the club's captain

I was part of the
club's back-to-back
promotion-winning teams
of 1986/87 and 1987/88

Since ending my playing
days I have returned to the
club for a spell as manager

I'm currently managing
a Championship rival

5. WHO AM I?

6. WHO AM I?

Leeds United were the first
English club I played for

I joined Boro in 2004
from Chelsea

I marked my Boro debut
with a goal against
Newcastle United

The 2006 UEFA Cup final
was my last game for Boro

I was capped 23 times
by the Netherlands during
my playing career

A real Riverside favourite, Juninho is widely regarded as one of the greatest players to have donned a Middlesbrough shirt in the modern era. Signed by Bryan Robson in October 1995, the Brazilian magician became a cult hero with the Boro faithful across three spells at the club.

A talented playmaker, Juninho starred in his debut campaign and then played a vital role as Boro reached the League Cup and FA Cup finals in 1997. After moving on to Atletico Madrid he returned to Teesside on loan in the 1999/2000 campaign.

Boro's prodigal son then returned to the club on a permanent basis in the summer of 2002 and helped the team win its first domestic cup competition when they landed the League Cup in 2004.

JUNINHO

BOROHEROES

EYE FOR AN OPENING

Not only was Juninho extremely comfortable on the ball but he also showed great vision and awareness on the pitch. He appeared to have the perfect eye for a quick pass to help Boro mount another attack.

QUICK FEET

Naturally blessed with exceptional close control and dribbling skills, Juninho had the ability to jinx his way past opponents and into dangerous areas. Always indentified as the dangerman, Juninho proved to be a tricky player for opposition to get to grips with.

INTELLIGENCE

A player's football intelligence is often spoken about and Juninho had it in abundance. He had the skill of making time on the ball, orchestrating the pattern of play and playing creative forward balls. He also had that ability of knowing the runs a teammate would make and the ability to find them with the minimum of fuss.

ADVICE

In his final spell at the Riverside, Juninho used his vast experience and knowledge gained from playing at the top level for club and country to help nurture the younger players in the Boro squad.

UCHE IKPEAZU

FAST FORWARD >>

Do your predictions for 2021/22 match our own?...

CHAMPIONSHIP WINNERS

Middlesbrough

CHAMPIONSHIP TOP SCORER

Uche Ikpeazu

CHAMPIONSHIP RUNNERS-UP

Fulham

CHAMPIONSHIP PLAY-OFF WINNERS

Reading

FA CUP WINNERS

Brighton & Hove Albion

FA CUP RUNNERS-UP

Leeds United

LEAGUE CUP WINNERS

Arsenal

LEAGUE CUP RUNNERS-UP

Leicester City

PREMIER LEAGUE WINNERS
Manchester United

PREMIER LEAGUE RUNNERS-UP
Chelsea

PREMIER LEAGUE TOP SCORER
Anthony Martial

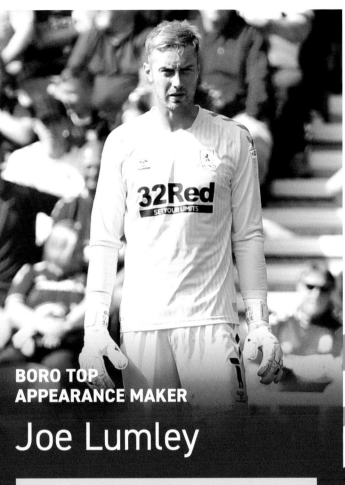

BORO TOP APPEARANCE MAKER
Joe Lumley

BORO PLAYER OF THE YEAR
Martin Payero

CHAMPIONS LEAGUE WINNERS
Barcelona

CHAMPIONS LEAGUE RUNNERS-UP
Real Madrid

EUROPA LEAGUE WINNERS
West Ham United

EUROPA LEAGUE RUNNERS-UP
Lazio

ANSWERS

PAGE 11
SOCCER SEARCH

Bicycle Kick.

PAGE 14
CLASSIC FANTASTIC

PAGE 26
GUESS THE CLUB

1. Newcastle United. 2. Wigan Athletic. 3. Leeds United.
4. Charlton Athletic. 5. Coventry City. 6. AFC Wimbledon.
7. Liverpool. 8. Millwall. 9.Wolverhampton Wanderers.
10. Nottingham Forest.

PAGE 48
ODD BALLS

1. Sunderland, C. 2. Portsmouth, C. 3. Arsenal, B.
4. Crewe Alexandra, A. 5. Queens Park Rangers, C.
6. Crystal Palace, B. 7. Tottenham Hotspur, B.
8. Reading, B. 9. Birmingham City, C.
10. West Ham United, D.

PAGE 56
GUESS WHO?

1. Stewart Downing. 2. Darren Randolph.
3. Ben Gibson. 4. Stuart Ripley.
5. Tony Mowbray. 6. Jimmy Floyd Hasselbaink.